Thank you for always
sharing great pearls
of wisdom & encouraging
me to do my best.

Love,

Jayne 9/26/15

Joyce L. Kyles

Restoring the Whole in My Soul

by Joyce L. Kyles

Joyce L. Kyles

Restoring the Whole
In My Soul

Copyright © 2015
Joyce L. Kyles

ISBN 13: 978-1511762380

Cover Photo @Audria Richmond,
AudriaRichmond.com
All rights reserved

Cover Photo Design @Jason Kyles
All rights reserved

Printed in the United States of America
By *CreateSpace*

DEDICATION

This book is dedicated with love and gratitude to the following:

- The Most High God. Without His love, grace, mercy, guidance, and infinite wisdom, I would not be able to understand and appreciate my life and purpose. I am forever grateful for where I've been, where I am, and where I'm going on this ever-changing journey called life.

- My husband, Jason L. Kyles. I love you and thank you for helping me to feel comfortable enough to trust in the concept of marriage. Our minds, bodies, and spirits are in complete unity with one another. I know that I am loved, respected, and supported. I am grateful for our friendship and like-minded faith, as they are the foundation of our union.

- My children, Carlotta, TaMara and TJ. I will never be able to put into words just how much I truly love you. We have been through a lot of joy and pain. We have laughed and cried. We have had many trials and triumphs. Despite it all, we've done it together. It is my honor to be your mother. It is my desire that you learn from my successes and failures. All of you are my inspiration and motivation. Thank you for supporting this journey and for the 'little people.'

- My family members, friends, colleagues, and acquaintances. There are too many of you to name. I am especially thankful and appreciative for the reasons, seasons, or lifetimes associated with our connections. It is extremely humbling to know that so many people care about me, my family, and my purpose.

- And, to the memory of my father, John Louis Spencer, Sr.; paternal grandmother, Edna Spencer; and maternal grandmother, Elsie Langford.

INTRODUCTION

Restoring the Whole in My Soul takes you on a resilient journey through the peaks and valleys of a survivor of domestic violence and sexual assault. While its primary influence stems from those adversities, this book provides an interesting read for addressing additional challenges that weaken, break, and destroy our mental and physical selves; those things that leave us in a state of hopelessness and despair. *Restoring the Whole in My Soul* offers practical and relatable experiences that have resulted in realistic strategies to acquire and retain a sense of holistic healing, self-reflection, self-sufficiency, forgiveness, and love. After each chapter, you will find a page for '**Restoration Notes**' which can be used for journaling purposes. This is a book about replacing, rebuilding, and reclaiming the pieces of your life while restoring your life to one of peace, prosperity, and purpose.

Joyce L. Kyles

Table of Contents

Restoring the Whole in My Soul

Joyce L. Kyles

Restoring the Whole in my Soul

I have two pairs of shoes I had considered throwing away. Both pairs are in pretty good shape overall. On the basic brown pair, one of the heels had completely disconnected from the base of the shoe. The other pair is shoe boots. They are designed with various models' faces and have names of cities printed on them. They are a rather eclectic pair of shoes, but both shoe taps have been worn down to the base of the heels.

I actually like both pairs. I didn't *really* want to get rid of them, but as I have done with toxic relationships, I felt it was necessary to accept that no matter how much I liked them or felt I needed them, it was time to let them go. I couldn't afford to buy new shoes, but I also couldn't afford to keep wearing either pair based on their condition. They were uncomfortable, unattractive, and clearly needed repair. Because of the fabric and materials used to make the shoes, repairing them seemed to be a far more expensive option.

Restoring the Whole in My Soul

I mentioned this to my now-husband. He took the shoes, thoroughly looked them over, and then suggested I take them to a shoe repair shop rather than simply throw them away. He felt I should allow an expert to look at them to determine whether or not they could be saved.

I was very reluctant at first. It wasn't that I didn't trust my husband. For me, it was more about knowing I had owned these shoes for a long time. I knew how they looked and felt on my feet when they were in a better condition. While they still appeared to have some spark of life, I believed they had arrived at a point beyond economic repair. Personally, I didn't see any significant value in them any longer. However, after a few days of thinking it over, I decided to take them to a local shoe repair shop for *at least* an inspection.

Joyce L. Kyles

When I arrived, I asked the store owner if he could look at the shoes and tell me if they were repairable. Of course, I was prepared to hear him say, "No way!" I would then be able to return home and tell my husband I was right all along. *Instead*, the owner quickly looked over both pairs of shoes, confirmed they were certainly repairable, and informed me that I could pick them up in a few days. In addition, the costs for the repairs were significantly cheaper than I could have *ever* imagined.

Within a few days, I was informed that my shoes were ready. I eagerly made my way to retrieve them. I paid for the repairs and quickly made my way back to the car so I could truly appreciate my shoes. I examined them and was pleasantly surprised to see they had been restored to look almost brand new! I could still see *small* scuffs here and there from general wear and tear. However, the heels – which represent the foundation of the shoes – were new, sturdy, and clean. They were able to again provide the necessary balance for me to walk upright.

Restoring the Whole in My Soul

I could now walk in confidence and without embarrassment. The small scuffs aren't really noticeable at all. A person would really have to work **hard** to find them. I'm sure I'm the only one who notices them because they are *my* shoes. They are *my* scuffmarks. I'm glad I didn't throw them away. I'm glad I listened to my husband's advice to have them repaired.

Joyce L. Kyles

Lessons Learned

For those of us who experienced abuse (or any other adversities, for that matter), it is very common to feel like the shoes I described. Have **you** ever felt broken and bruised? Have **you** ever looked in the mirror and didn't like the person you saw? Or maybe you're among the number of those who can't even bear to look at themselves at all.

When I was living as a victim, my mental instability began to manifest itself in the way I walked, talked, and dressed. I avoided others at times – including my children. I felt I was beyond repair. I certainly didn't *see* myself as attractive. I was convinced that no one would take me seriously. I felt thrown away and worthless. I felt that whatever value I **may** have had was no longer in existence. I spent so much time pointing out my scars, I didn't recognize the beauty and usefulness that still remained within me. My foundation had been *rocked*. For years, it had been deteriorating. One day, it finally gave way, and the entire base had been completely knocked out from under me.

Restoring the Whole in My Soul

There is a happy ending, though. Someone was able to see past my brokenness and convince me that I could be restored to a place of peace and wholeness by providing me encouragement and guidance. My foundation has now been restored and repaired. I will always have some scars from what I've been through, but those experiences do **not** define me.

I wear suits and heels. I pay strict attention to holding my head up, shoulders back, and walking with confidence. I am grateful there was someone who took an interest in me, supported me, and helped to develop my sense of self-worth and respect. My children encouraged me and are not ashamed of me. I now feel like my shoes. I have a *few* scuffs, but my basic personality, sense of style, and humor are more visible because my foundation has been restored. I look in the mirror and love my reflection. Beauty is more than just what is aesthetically appealing; it is about inner-strength, perseverance, and resiliency.

Joyce L. Kyles

I am aesthetically attractive because I do not allow others' definition of what beautiful is define who I am. That definition changes from person to person. Therefore, I will not be mentally enslaved to that imagery because I would constantly find myself changing to accommodate others.

Restoring the Whole in My Soul

RESTORATION NOTES

_____

_____

_____

_____

_____

_____

_____

_____

_____

_____

_____

_____

_____

_____

_____

_____

_____

_____

_____

_____

_____

_____

_____

_____

_____

_____

_____

Joyce L. Kyles

On a Suicide Mission

There have been many times in my life when I felt there was no hope. I had no answers. I had no clue how to keep going. None have been as profound as the night I made the decision to take my own life. I'm not going to be one of those people who will tell you that I regret feeling that way back then. The truth is: I *don't* regret it. In the moment, I felt I had all the right reasons to feel the way I did.

The man I loved at the time – my now ex-husband – told me he should just kill me. He then went on to choke and rape me without a care that I was pregnant at the time. I was without a car and job. I was living with relatives. I was without hope and self-esteem. I had $50.00 in food stamps and a measly $3.00 in cash to my name. Given the same set of circumstances at that point in my life, I can now better understand why I felt that dying was my best and **only** solution.

*I **do** have one regret, however; I regret the position I placed myself in where I felt ending my life was the **only** option.*

Restoring the Whole in My Soul

I was told by others that I needed to leave, but no one actually told me *how* to do it. I was told I deserved better, but I didn't understand what **better** looked and felt like. Leaving is not as easy as it seems. When you've been holistically broken down and made to feel hopeless, *better* merely meant not hurting anymore. At that time in my life, **better** for me meant *death*.

I didn't know then what I know now. Counseling was not something I even thought about. I had not heard of any family members or friends who had gone through that process. I wasn't encouraged by those who knew my situation to reach out and get counseled. I grew up during the time when people believed what happens in the home, stays in the home. Basically, you found a way to live through "*it*". You kept "*it*" quiet. You prayed about "*it*". You did **everything** but talk about "*it*". Talking about "*it*" has the potential to destroy personal and professional relationships. What if you're not believed at all? What if you **are** believed, but were directly (or indirectly) told it's not as bad as you *said* it was?

Those were the issues I experienced during that time. Because I have chosen the path of advocacy, I have since learned I was not alone in my experiences. I've also made a point of making sure I educate others on what to expect before, during, and after they leave an unhealthy relationship. If you are someone who's gone through adversities such as homelessness, poverty, cancer, etc., you will likely go through some variation of those same experiences.

I initially believed that if I died, someone more fitting would take care of my children. I didn't feel like I was a fit enough person to care for them because I wasn't able to take care of myself. I didn't like myself, and I certainly didn't **love** myself. I believed *some* people would miss me, but they would eventually get over their hurt.

So, are you wondering why I didn't go through with committing suicide?

Restoring the Whole in My Soul

The one aspect of my life that has remained consistent is my belief that a spirit of higher power dwells within me. I am convinced that it dwells within *all* of us. That relationship should be intimate, personal, nurtured, and protected. It was that inner-voice that convinced me killing myself would either kill my unborn child or cause my child to suffer from deformities as a result of my actions. *I didn't have the right to do that.* I'm glad I listened to that inner-voice. I'm honored to be a mother. I'm grateful that my life was spared and that I was given another chance to get myself together.

Joyce L. Kyles

Lessons Learned

The older I get, the more I recognize that when I move away from daily prayer, meditation, and reading, I allow myself to become more vulnerable. It leads to an emotional door I unintentionally leave wide open for negative energies and opportunities to take root. I expose my spiritual nakedness to the world while allowing the world to clothe me in its wickedness, ill-will, unhealthy agendas, and mental anguish.

Every difficult situation I face is another opportunity to exercise my faith-factor. I don't just mean faith in the spiritual sense. I mean having faith in *myself*. I mean having faith in the *system*. I mean having faith in *strangers*. I mean having faith in my *family* and *friends*. Faith is so much more than the ability to believe in a higher spiritual power. I believe faith is a mindset that says, "I believe in my faith to endure, overcome, and be holistically successful." I believe in the power of resiliency and efficiency. I have enough faith in what I see and hear to make sound and informed decisions that are healthy, safe, engaging, and beneficial to my overall well-being.

Restoring the Whole in My Soul

RESTORATION NOTES

_____

_____

_____

_____

_____

_____

_____

_____

_____

_____

_____

_____

_____

_____

_____

_____

_____

_____

_____

_____

_____

_____

_____

_____

Joyce L. Kyles

Preparing for the Worst

As bad as my contemplation of suicide was, it still wasn't as bad as the place I put myself in years later when I remarried. I didn't think I would ever truly recover. I thought my children would never forgive me. Physical abuse can leave visibly permanent scars. It can also leave temporary scars that heal over time, such as a black eye or busted mouth. Over the course of time, you may even forget about it or your feelings regarding the abuse's severity may fade.

One major difference between my first marriage and the second was that there was only one instance of physical abuse that took place during the second, and we had been married for several years when it happened. Looking back on it now, I believe the only reason it never happened again had more to do with the police being called. As well, some of his family members were made aware of what happened. It was outright embarrassing for him. I have never believed it never happened again because he viewed it as wrong.

Restoring the Whole in My Soul

I mentioned previously that I am now an abuse advocate. When I train, I tell attendees about the variety of abuses - many which include physical, mental, emotional, sexual, financial, religious, and social trauma. Although I dealt with all of those issues in my first marriage to a certain degree, it was my *second* marriage that would prove to be worse because **that** husband *knew* the traumas I experienced in the first marriage. I feel as though he used a lot of that information against me. He used my fear of failure, embarrassment, desire to keep my family together, and my overall lack of confidence to do and say things that hurt me – which, in turn, hurt my children. So, while he didn't physically attack me to the point of broken limbs and physical impairments, he attacked my *mind*.

I didn't understand at the time that I was being abused. Neither did he believe he was being abusive. I know this because I've talked to him since our break-up about different issues that took place during our marriage. He has never apologized. Instead, he explained why his actions were justified.

I actually knew *at least* five years prior to me actually leaving my second marriage for good that I needed to get out of that relationship. In addition to all of the issues I faced in my first marriage, I had to address the fact that I was in a failed relationship for a second time. The parental figures in my life – my father and paternal grandmother – were both deceased at that point in time. Before then, when I needed someone to talk to, I could talk to them. I didn't tell them *everything*, but I could rest assured they would give me some solid answers based on what I did share, and I **knew** that I would be made to feel better.

I was too embarrassed to share with anyone else what was happening to me. The one time I gathered up enough courage to reach out to someone, I quickly realized that disclosing we were in "trouble" was also opening me up to scrutiny and questions I couldn't answer. It would be the same questions I had no answers for in the past when asked by others. *I didn't know why I was still there. I didn't know why I allowed my family to live in an environment that wasn't safe inside or out.*

Restoring the Whole in My Soul

What a difference time and education have made in my life. When I understood that excessive arguing, name-calling, making decisions regarding intimacy, and other issues were not nuances to be expected as a part of marriage, but rather, it was a way of enforcing abuse, I began to slowly take ownership over my life and realized just how unhappy I was. I began to understand why I was still in a place that I didn't belong. I also began to understand why it was important to leave – *no matter what*.

Yes, I considered myself to be relatively smart. I had a college degree that proved helpful in my professional life. However, my degree did not address my personal needs. I didn't look for or expect it to do so. As I look back now, there are some courses I took that could have actually been useful to reflect on regarding my personal development. At the time, none of that seemed relevant because, as I said, I didn't have a good understanding about the signs of abuse; therefore, I didn't see myself as a victim.

I feel that it's also appropriate to note that my first husband wrote me a letter several years ago. Even though he tried to justify some of his actions, he apologized and said that he didn't remember everything that had occurred. He did, however, remember enough to know that he had hurt me and the children.

Restoring the Whole in My Soul

Lessons learned

Restoration in this chapter was, for me, two-fold. I've had to learn forgiveness. I've had to learn to take responsibility and accountability for my part in the turmoil that took place in those relationships. Self-reflection is one of the hardest things to do (in my opinion) because it forces you to do a critical analysis of yourself. That's not easy. I didn't want to admit that my relationship choices were a reflection of what I thought was normal.

I'd seen people argue and fight in their marriages and relationships, and those people were still together – or if they *had* broken up, I didn't consider that it had to do with abuse. I have worked since I was 16 years old, so I've always had the idea of me taking care of me. When I began to have children, that concept became me taking care of them. It didn't matter to me if my parent partner worked or not. I knew I would always do my best to take care of everything regardless of the situation. I believed that once you married, you were married for life. I never considered any aspect about marrying someone and not being compatible in mind and spirit.

Admittedly, my first husband and I were too young and going in different directions when we got married. I should have never allowed myself to think I could change him or believe that I wouldn't change. At age 18, you think you can do anything with love and support. He broke me down in a way I didn't come to terms with until many years later when I attended a seminar where I learned about Post Traumatic Stress Disorder – commonly known as PTSD. Learning about PTSD helped explain why certain actions would trigger negative impulses and tremors that (previously) I couldn't explain.

Restoring the Whole in My Soul

With regard to the second marriage, I saw the red flags immediately while explaining them away. We didn't argue the same way as in my first marriage. Even though it was bad, in my mind, it wasn't *as* bad as the potential of being slapped or pushed into a wall. I used my tongue as a weapon because I knew I couldn't win a physical confrontation against him. I was comfortable and accustomed to independently taking care of a household and living without a man. Since he wasn't physically violent and I didn't really acknowledge anything else he did as being abusive, I didn't have a problem with arguing. I didn't mind my children hearing some of the things I said to and about him to his face. I wanted them to see me as strong, but it had the opposite effect. I was being abusive to him as well, and my children were caught in the crossfire. Leaving the relationship for good also meant that I would need to restore my children's faith in me as their protector, nurturer, and provider of their basic needs. I would have to regain their trust. It took quite some time for that to happen, but eventually it did.

Joyce L. Kyles

RESTORATION NOTES

_____

_____

_____

_____

_____

_____

_____

_____

_____

_____

_____

_____

_____

_____

_____

_____

_____

_____

_____

_____

_____

_____

_____

_____

_____

_____

_____

Restoring the Whole in My Soul

Love after Abuse

I was a caseworker who provided direct services for clients at least ½ of each day. One day in particular, I walked to the customer service desk like I'd done almost every day to sign in a client I was expecting. Suddenly, I heard a male voice nearby say, "Excuse me. Can you help me?" I didn't even look in his direction. *In my defense, I must mention this: At the place where I worked, people were often stopping the workers to ask questions and plead their case rather than following protocol.* Instead of turning to face the man, I responded – in a very curt tone – "Hold on just a minute", and continued signing in the date and time of my client's consult.

When I *did* turn around, I found myself looking up at this tall, handsome, well-dressed man with *beautiful* eyes. My disenchantment for being interrupted quickly turned into delight. I smiled and asked him what he needed. He returned the smile and stated that he was looking for an individual who was actually one of my managers. Because I had a client waiting for me, I didn't want to engage the gentleman too long – but at the same time, I didn't want *anyone else* to assist him. He was attractive. He smelled great. His smile was pleasant and friendly. If only for a few minutes, I wanted to exist in the presence of this man's energy.

Almost a year prior, I had left my husband. I was convinced I would never give my heart to anyone ever again. I purposely made it a point to not notice men or engage them in conversation outside of casually speaking. That day was the first time in a **long** time I had really looked at a man and thought, "*Dang, he's fine!*" Even as I write about that day now, I'm finding myself blushing. On that day, I had a difficult one up to that point, and he was truly a breath of fresh air.

Restoring the Whole in My Soul

I told my client I would be right back and attempted to locate the manager for this man. Unfortunately, I was unable to find him. At that point, he stated he would try another time. When I asked if he wanted to leave a card, he declined, thanked me for my assistance, and left the building. Two of my co-workers asked me who he was and if I had gotten his name or phone number. I answered their questions and we joked about him being '*fine*'. That was the end of it, and I never expected to see him again.

When I saw my manager the next day and described the man to him, he immediately knew who I was referring to. He said his name was Jason Kyles. He shared a bit about Jason, his family, and the kind of work he was doing as it related to them meeting with one another. I found the person he was describing to be interesting. With the jokes about him **NOT** having a wife, I'm sure I was blushing (though it was not intentional).

Joyce L. Kyles

I am a visual person. As my manager was talking, I was reflecting back on the day before and remembering how nice the man smelled. Again, with all that was said, I *STILL* didn't think I would ever see him again. Even if I did, I wasn't even slightly interested in trying to get to know him in a romantic way. However, I did think he may be a good fit for a project I was working on with an organization I was connected to at the time. *I didn't share any of that with my manager, though. It was just a passing thought.*

About a week later, as I was returning from lunch – late, mind you – my friend/colleague in customer service tells me there is someone waiting to see me. I was baffled because I didn't have any clients scheduled…which was why I wasn't especially concerned about my late return. I looked around and told her the only person I saw was the man who's been looking for our manager. She responded, "That's who's here to see you." At that point, I thought to myself, "What for?" Nonetheless, I went over to speak with him.

Restoring the Whole in My Soul

As it turned out, the same colleague asked him to stay around because I needed to see him. It was at that point we both realized we had been set up. I was so embarrassed and unsure of what to say. Thinking about the project I was currently working on, I thought I would use the opportunity to tell him about it. As for why we were being set up, I decided I would find out about that later.

I invited him to my office to chat and soon realized he wasn't the right person for the program for which I was serving as Co-Chair. However, the conversation *was* interesting and informative. We discovered we had several things in common and had complimentary skills that could prove to be mutually-beneficial in moving some business ideas forward. We agreed to meet that coming weekend.

After he left, I asked my colleague why she had obviously set us up. Her response was that he seemed like a nice man and that she thought if anyone deserved to be with a nice man, it was me. Again: I wasn't *interested* in being with a man at that time.

Joyce L. Kyles

In addition to my disinterest in a relationship, we'd just been informed that our agency would not be receiving grant funding for the next fiscal year and we were going to be laid off in a couple of months. I was only interested in trying to figure out where my family was going to live and how I was going to afford food, clothing, and shelter for myself and my children.

*I was, however, appreciative that my colleague thought enough of me to do what she did. I appreciated that she thought enough of **him** to believe that he was the type of man who would treat **me** the way I deserved to be treated.*

After that initial weekend meeting and over the course of the following five years, Jason Kyles would go on to help me start my own business, encourage me to use my voice to help others, and assist me with the establishment of a grassroots movement that has since become a non-profit organization.

Restoring the Whole in My Soul

One of the most important things Jason ever said to me was early on in our friendship. He told me I was a beautiful, smart, and intelligent woman with a good heart, but I acted like I had been through something. His comment made me **very** angry. I hadn't known him long enough at the time for me not to feel as though his comment was unsolicited and out of place. It did, however, make me take a long, hard look at myself.

What did *others* see when they looked at me?

I did, after all, walk with my head down. I didn't make a great deal of eye contact. My shoulders were hunched up all the time. I rubbed on my arms – **a lot**. Jason provided me an honesty I didn't want but certainly needed.

After years of personal and professional twists and turns, our friendship blossomed into a beautiful courtship. It would be another year and a half before we officially exchanged wedding vows.

Lessons Learned

Anyone who sees me today never questions whether or not I'm happy or if I love my husband. They can see it in the way I blush whenever his name is mentioned. They can hear it when I talk about him for any length of time. Jason gave me the love, safety, and confidence to believe that it was alright to trust another human being with my heart. He offered me his last name. I am honored to be Mrs. Jason Kyles.

Also, I have come to appreciate the concept of self-love. Going forward, I plan on never being that frail, timid individual I was a few years ago.

Not to get ahead here, I will discuss restoring one's inner- and outer-self in another chapter.

Restoring the Whole in My Soul

The idea of love after abuse can be scary, but it can happen and should be explored – when you're **ready**. Exactly when that happens is different for everyone. Although there was a bit of match-making taking place, I still didn't force the relationship. It happened naturally and unexpectedly. We developed a friendship and established trust. Even though I found myself attracted to him aesthetically, I could not immediately appreciate my feelings for him or trust my sense of understanding as to whether or not those feelings were based on lust or love.

As I began to understand myself, I was able to put things in perspective and mend the pieces of my heart that had previously been bruised. I had grown to realize I didn't need to stay in an unhealthy relationship out of embarrassment or fear of being alone. Most importantly, I understood I didn't need to be in a *romantic relationship* to make me feel complete.

Joyce L. Kyles

RESTORATION NOTES

_____

_____

_____

_____

_____

_____

_____

_____

_____

_____

_____

_____

_____

_____

_____

_____

_____

_____

_____

_____

_____

_____

_____

_____

_____

Restoring the Whole in My Soul

Unrequited & Self Love

Most of us – at one time or another – have experienced unrequited love. Unrequited love is when the love you feel for someone is not returned. In some cases, it is because one person may not even be aware of the other person's feelings. An example of this would be a secret crush. Rarely will you find a person who's in a hurry to deal with rejection or making a friendly relationship awkward. As such, if there's even a *hint* of putting that relationship in jeopardy, a person may choose to keep his or her true feelings inside.

In other cases, the person who is the object of someone's affection **is** well aware of the other's feelings. The person in love has expressed his or her feelings in some way that leaves no room for doubt regarding their heart. It is a huge risk on the part of the person in love. Expressing those feelings puts them in a vulnerable position of openness and, again, there is always the *possibility* of rejection, embarrassment, and awkwardness.

In the past, when I thought of love in that way, I didn't necessarily equate it with domestic abuse. However, I have since come to believe that I've dealt with unrequited love in its truest form.

One of the biggest errors I ever made was putting all of my love, attention, and affection into a partner who did not love, care for, or respect me. I loved my partners coupled with the illusion of my relationships – more than I loved myself. I enjoyed being married and what the institute of marriage represented. I desperately wanted those same feelings to be reciprocated. I found myself holding on to the idea of being loved, even though I knew the relationship I desired was only in my head.

Restoring the Whole in My Soul

Let me make this clear: If a man or woman loves you, they will not hit you. They will not belittle or disrespect you. He or she will support your dreams and aspirations. He or she will offer guidance and constructive criticism. They will not be ashamed of you – neither will they do anything that would cause you to be ashamed of them. Love is an action word for which bullying, degradation, sexual assault, illness, unforeseen tragedies, or abuses of any form play no part in its ability to be given freely and unconditionally.

Joyce L. Kyles

Lessons Learned

As I began to love and respect myself, I grew to understand the relationships I thought I had didn't really exist. I was fearful of leaving, in part, because I was afraid of losing my family unit. I wanted to keep the *appearance* of a loving, caring household. I was living a fantasy that was hard to let go of. Once I did let go, the truth of my situation placed my reality on full display.

As a human being, I enjoy the company and companionship of others. There's nothing wrong with that; it is a healthy part of living. However, when that need requires that I sacrifice my emotional safety, it is time to reexamine my definition of love and self-worth to see if it's truly in alignment with the relationships I am now involved in – whether personal or professional.

Establishing a true love for self will help establish boundaries of what you will and will not accept in a relationship. I had to remove my name from the pity-party guest list. The ability to love is a beautiful quality to have. The key to remaining happy has been protecting my heart so that love is given and received not only in the way I desire, but also the way I know I deserve.

Restoring the Whole in My Soul

RESTORATION NOTES

_____

_____

_____

_____

_____

_____

_____

_____

_____

_____

_____

_____

_____

_____

_____

_____

_____

_____

_____

_____

_____

_____

_____

_____

_____

_____

_____

Joyce L. Kyles

Get Over Yourself

Our physical and emotional functionality is contingent upon what we put in our bodies. Personally, I am a huge fan of sweets. I love butter cookies, chocolate, and peach cobbler. I also enjoy cheesecake – and I have a good friend who makes some of the **best** homemade cheesecake I have *ever* eaten in my **life**. Sadly, I have been guilty (more times than I care to share) of over-indulging in those things. As a matter-of-fact, I've been told on at least three occasions by physicians that chocolate (in particular) is not good for me to consume because I have issues with acne.

If it is true that the definition of insanity is doing the same thing over and over again while expecting a different result, then it is no wonder I still find myself struggling with weight loss and gain. To this very day, I will go to the grocery store to buy fruit, but still haven't mastered enough discipline to push my cart past the ice cream section without rationalizing how my strawberries would complement it to perfection.

Restoring the Whole in My Soul

Just as a healthy body cannot be achieved and maintained by eating unhealthy foods and over-indulging, a positive spirit cannot dwell in a negative host. Most of the time when I would say a person needs to get over himself or herself, I would be referring to someone who, as I like to say, has an exaggerated sense of one's own importance. That statement is not to be confused with a person who has a high regard for who they are. There's nothing wrong with having self-confidence. I'm talking about those individuals who teeter on the borderline or have crossed the line of conceit. I have lived with them. I have worked with them. If you take a moment, I'm sure you can think of at least one person who fits that description.

I, however, spent a large amount of time in my life feeling the total opposite. I didn't feel I was good enough. In high school, I had friends and, for the most part, I was well-liked. I was never able to achieve being part of the ultimate 'in crowd' that seemed to be so very important during those crucial teen years. As an adult, I've always been able to acknowledge beautiful, intelligent, and successful women. However, I did not see myself in the same way. I could not seem to get past viewing myself as 'average'. I couldn't seem to view myself as being better and, more importantly, *deserving* better.

I've learned that just as some people need to get over themselves in terms of thinking they are **the most** beautiful or handsome or **the** smartest or **most** gifted, it is equally important to get over the mindset that your circumstances have to dictate your future. I am **not** a victim of circumstance. Outer beauty is completely overrated. What is beautiful to me may be completely unattractive to the next person. How many of us can think of someone as absolutely stunning aesthetically, but he or she is shallow, superficial, and condescending in his or her speech and attitude towards others?

Restoring the Whole in My Soul

Society continues to dictate what is considered beautiful and what success should look like. If I had continued to buy into it, I would always be average – and there's *nothing* average about me. I am unique, special, and created the way God intended. Who am I to insult Him by suggesting that I'm average based on what others' definition of belonging and self-worth means to them?

Over the last few years, I have a flat mole that has grown to spread across a portion of the left side of my face. It starts just under my eye and comes down a portion of my cheek. I absolutely cannot stand it! Depending on the lighting when I'm taking pictures or appearing on television, it looks really dark and has made me uncomfortable. Before we were married, Jason shared with me that while he thinks I'm pretty with or without glasses, he prefers that I not wear them. What he *doesn't* know is that the biggest reason I wore my glasses was to help hide the mole. (*If he says something to me about this, then I'll know he's read my book!*)

I actually prefer to wear contact lenses. I still do, but I do not have the same outlook as I did about the reason initially. I alternate between my glasses and contact lenses for the sake of my eyes and not because I'm hiding the mole behind the glasses. However, I still don't like this mole and may eventually have it removed – not because of what others think of it one way or the other, but because, as I've said previously, I can't stand it! Regardless, whether it stays or goes, I am still my beautiful, wonderful, courageous, ambition self – and I'm holistically happy.

Restoring the Whole in My Soul

Lessons Learned

Before I could begin the process of becoming holistically restored, I first had to understand the degree at which I was broken. I also had to come to accept some responsibility and accountability in my life. I had to see myself where I was **and** as I was. I had to take each day as it came and see myself as great – no matter what the day brought my way. I had to see all opportunities and experiences as teachable moments as things that would either break my spirit or my cycle of adversities. Happiness and the ability to survive and thrive takes work, skill, creativity, and an unshakable will to live a resilient life full of purpose, passion, and prosperity.

As a survivor, I now understand that my strength is in my voice. It's in my writings. It's in the way I walk and carry myself. Silence gives your abuser/aggressor undeserving control of your mind, body, and spirit. It's okay to walk away from a person, job, organization, church or religious group, friends, and yes, even family if you find yourself being compromised to the point of harm.

See, it doesn't matter what my aggressors have to say about me to whomever – whether they have been personal or professional in nature. There are three sides to every story. The person telling the story will definitely have a bias, and the overall character of the one telling the story should be taken into account – as well as the one being discussed.

Also, consider this: For some people, displaying an aura of confidence to the point of conceit and belittlement of others is also a sign of deeply-rooted insecurities that stem from adversities they have faced or are currently dealing with their own lives. It's a coping mechanism. It's a way to mask the hurt.

Part of restoration comes in the form of admitting you are unhappy. As for me, because I had such low self-esteem and lack of belief in just how holistically beautiful I am, I relied on my smile, animated story-telling, and dry, sarcastic humor to shield my hurts and pains. It worked many times. To this day, I come in contact with people who have heard me speak and they are amazed to know I was dealing with some of the issues for which I am offering training. *What usually happens next is someone tells me that it was their story or that they know of someone who has had a similar experience.*

Restoring the Whole in My Soul

RESTORATION NOTES

_____

_____

_____

_____

_____

_____

_____

_____

_____

_____

_____

_____

_____

_____

_____

_____

_____

_____

_____

_____

_____

_____

_____

Joyce L. Kyles

Talk to Yourself...Out Loud

How many times have you heard that it's alright to talk to yourself – as long as you don't answer back? It is perceived that if you answer back, you may have a mental disability of sorts. While that may be true for some, I am of the opinion that it's perfectly fine to answer yourself. In order to know what I wanted, I had to first ask myself *what* I wanted. I encourage you to talk to yourself and ask yourself what you want and need…out loud.

Why is it important to say things out loud? Imagine this: What I wanted had been kept silent for so long, I didn't know my own voice. I didn't know my own power. I didn't know what it meant to be assertive and have true ownership over my voice. I spent a good deal of my time screaming and yelling "at the top of my lungs" while trying to make other people hear what I had to say. Then, there were *other* times I was afraid to open my mouth and felt it was best to remain silent – not necessarily because of what someone may say or do to me; it had more to do with how I felt about myself and how the arguing made me feel physically sick and sad.

Restoring the Whole in My Soul

I quietly and carefully questioned myself more times than I can count. *How many times have I played over and over in my head the reasons I stayed in an unhealthy relationship or kept working at a job where I felt unappreciated and was unsatisfied? How many times did I go to worship service because it seemed like the right thing to do?*

Hearing my story in my own words and in my own voice is a powerful affirmation of growth, strength, and resiliency. Hearing what I actually sounded like when I was processing all that has happened allowed me to hear what others heard when I spoke. It allowed me to hear the nervousness, fear, anger, and disappointment that comes during the beginning stages of coming out of adversity. What it also provided was a way to start examining where I was and what I needed to do to build up my confidence and self-esteem. Speaking aloud gave me a chance to practice what I would say to people who would choose to ask me questions like, "Why did you stay?" or "Why didn't you tell anyone you had been sick?"

Anyone who's going through adversities or have gone through them should prepare themselves for questions the moment they make their situations known to the public. 'The public' includes family members, friends, service providers, and members of the clergy. *How will you sound to them? How do you sound to yourself?*

I used to tell my children that when the world has broken their hearts and stepped on their feelings, keep a positive voice and face until they made it back home. Then, they could go to the bathroom and cry their hearts out. "You can always come and cry to me," I would tell them.

Some other tactics that have worked for me were calling or visiting a friend or family member who made me feel physically and emotionally safe and allowed my emotions to flow. Want another idea? Try standing in front of a mirror while observing your facial expressions, hand gestures, and overall body language when you're preparing to go out to speak to others about your needs, wants, and desires.

Restoring the Whole in My Soul

What does your voice sound like to other people? The voice you use when you're angry is harbored and perceived as an angry feeling or emotion that is later dismissed when the arguing or abuse stops and the issue appears to have calmed down a bit. Therefore, your voice gets ignored and taken for granted. It's perceived that you only said or reacted the way you did because you were upset at the time.

When your agenda changes, your tone becomes more assertive, your walk is more self-assured, and you display confidence in yourself. You become a threat: You threaten others' abilities to mistreat you. That encompasses husbands, wives, co-workers, employers, children...*everyone*. That means telling the waiter your food wasn't prepared properly and to have the chef cook it again – rather than just accepting it because you don't want to cause any problems or make a scene.

Lessons learned

There are many things you can do to ensure your voice is heard in the way it's deserved and intended. While there are many examples you can add to the following list, I've found the ones mentioned have been the most effective for *me*.

- **Daily affirmations.** Every single day, tell yourself that you are beautiful/handsome and charming. Tell yourself that it's going to be a great day because you are here to see it. Find something about yourself that you like and play up to that 'thing' – that '**it**' that makes you, well... *YOU*!

I have gained an entirely different perspective about self-affirmations. In the beginning stages of transitioning out of my adversities, I found it extremely difficult to focus on anything positive about myself. I encourage you to think of something someone has shared with you that they considered to be a great feature about you. Maybe it's your eyes. Maybe it's your hair. Maybe you have a warm smile or pleasant personality.

The person who abused you noticed something about you that made him or her interested in you. If he/she noticed it, use that fact to tell yourself that someone else will notice it, too – with the difference being that someone new will not mistreat those special traits. Rather, they will embrace it with friendship, a partnership, or possibly even a relationship.

If homelessness was an issue, get some flowers (even if they're plastic) and place them in the window of your new home. If overcoming an illness was an issue, remind yourself each day that you're getting stronger. Remind yourself of the time when you couldn't do those things.

Again, don't just **think** them; *say them*. Give your words life! Believe in them. Speak them with confidence, knowing there will always be peaks and valleys.

Understand that each day is another affirmation: You are here. Your life matters. Your life has value and purpose.

Restoring the Whole in My Soul

- **Counseling.** Most cities offer individual and support group counseling for many types of adversities. Use the Internet to research local agencies and consider contacting places such as your local Red Cross, YWCA/YMCA, Department of Human Services, or Health Department – just to name a few. If you have a primary care physician, let him or her know that you're interested in joining a support group. Some may assess a fee, while others are absolutely free. Check with your local domestic violence agencies regarding various counseling option requirements to include (but not limited to): fees, insurance options, parking, transportation, and childcare availability.

Please don't dismiss the idea of counseling. So much can be learned about yourself when you surround yourself with those who have experienced the same challenges you have. It's also good to have an unbiased person who can give you a different outlook on your specific situation. Sometimes, even well-meaning friends and family can give you wrong or inadequate information. It's not their intent. The advice given by those closest to us tends to come from a biased perspective or it's based on their level of knowledge about issues they may not truly understand.

For example, my understanding about domestic violence is a lot different now than what it was several years ago. The advice I'd give someone today is a lot different than what I would have offered back then.

My intent would have been good, but my advice wouldn't have been as efficient.

Restoring the Whole in My Soul

- **Journals.** Keeping a journal is one of the single most important tools I could ever suggest to anyone, especially when you are in the early stages of leaving an abusive relationship or addressing an adversity of any type. You have a lot of emotions to deal with, and writing helps give those emotions a place to rest.

I lived in Chicago, Illinois as a child. When I was in elementary school, I had a wonderful teacher who encouraged us to write. She entered one of my writings into the Gwendolyn Brooks Poetry Contest. She always encouraged me to write about how I felt and praised my efforts of trying to be a good writer. In the 5th grade, I won my first city-wide writing contest. I will always be grateful to her for taking an interest in me and encouraging me to write. It has been extremely therapeutic, and I consider it a safe haven for my thoughts.

Another important part of my restoration has been looking back at some of the things I've written to see just how far I've come. I've been able to reflect on times when I thought I was beyond help, hope, or healing. However, as I read through the pages of my life and see the progress I've made, I am encouraged. I find strength. I see my growth and resilience. I see the ways in which I'm rebuilding my life.

What I also understand through my journaling is that I have a place of reference. If I should ever find myself going backwards or having a hard day, I have documented proof that I have gone through difficult challenges before, and by mercy, grace, and countless avenues of support, I lived through them all.

Restoring the Whole in My Soul

- **Vision boards.** As I've mentioned before, I am definitely a visual person. The great thing about creating a vision board is that it allowed me to restore my love of being creative while increasing my belief that I could attain the things I posted and had written.

It was important for me to see and know I could dream without ridicule, express my goals and desires through words and pictures, and live a life of expectancy that those things **will** come to fruition.

I highly suggest you make more than one vision board as time progresses. The first one I made was very simple. I only had a few things on it, and it was mostly in written form. The second time I created one, it had far more pictures of the vision where I saw myself, what I wanted to have, and where I wanted to go. It was **much** more detailed than the first one.

By the time I made the second board, I was at a different place in my life where my visions, goals, and expectations were different. I have yet to achieve *every single thing* on either board, and that has not been the most significant part of the process for me. The most significant part is that I dared to dream. I dared to share. I dared to **believe** I could do everything posted on my boards.

Restoring the Whole in My Soul

RESTORATION NOTES

_____

_____

_____

_____

_____

_____

_____

_____

_____

_____

_____

_____

_____

_____

_____

_____

_____

_____

_____

_____

_____

_____

_____

_____

_____

Joyce L. Kyles

The Joy of June

For the past several years, June was a horrible month for me to deal with. My second marriage ended in June. I was laid off from my job in June. I endured an illness in June. I'm sure if I thought about it some more, I could name some other incidences. Every year, I feared its arrival because I just *knew* that **something** bad was going to happen. I found myself having to relocate every year in June.

I had even arrived at the point where I was starting to brace myself months in advance for June's impending arrival. There had been nothing especially positive about that month. I expected the worst. I would even venture to say that I *looked* for the worst. It had become instinctive. As such, when unpleasant events took place, I wasn't the least bit surprised.

Restoring the Whole in My Soul

Lessons learned

I had to find a way to restore my mind to think of June as a month of joy. As I began to rebuild my life, I simply decided not to think of June as a month of grief, but rather as one of growth. I began to examine each situation and allowed myself to take inventory of the lessons I had learned. I made a conscious decision to find *something* positive. As I began to think things through, I established two important points:

1. I lived through them all. It was not easy – and I certainly didn't always do it with poise and style – but I made it.

2. There **were** some good things that happened in June.

Due to my broken mindset, I found myself dwelling on everything else that appeared to be broken and filled with despair. Yes, I had moved several times over the years, but the last time I moved, it was because I wanted to – not because I had to. Yes, my second marriage ended in June and, ironically, my divorce became final several years to the date of our separation – but the separation was the beginning of my holistic freedom. The divorce itself brought me a sense of closure I desperately needed and desired.

I purposefully completed writing my book in June. I wanted to add something positive to the growing list of things I have discovered about the beauty and joy of June. I wanted to create a sense of balance. I am aware that things can happen any given day at any given time. Oftentimes, those things are beyond our control anyway. I decided I no longer want to stay enslaved to a negative mindset. As I mentioned before, *a positive spirit cannot dwell in a negative host*.

Restoring the Whole in My Soul

RESTORATION NOTES

_____

_____

_____

_____

_____

_____

_____

_____

_____

_____

_____

_____

_____

_____

_____

_____

_____

_____

_____

_____

_____

_____

Joyce L. Kyles

Let the Restoration Begin

I gave birth to three beautiful children; two daughters and a son. They were each born at different times of the day and night – and in different seasons. They are physically different in their complexions, height, and overall body composition. For instance, my oldest daughter is the shortest. My son is the youngest. My middle daughter has a section of hair that grows as a very light bronze. There is a gap of a few years between the birth of my oldest and other two, as the last two were born very close together. They have three completely different personalities. At times, those personalities have been some of *the most* challenging experiences to endure as their mother. Still, they have also been some of the most rewarding experiences I could have ever been blessed to have. I wouldn't trade my three amigos for anything in the world.

Restoring the Whole in My Soul

Everyone's experience with trauma is different. Therefore, one's reaction to it will be different as well. How we view ourselves is different, too. If you've been told that you're fat or unattractive while believing that ultimate beauty is that of society's standard version of a supermodel, you will remain in a broken state of mind. That mental tape recorder of you being told those negative things will continue to take precedence over the truth: *Beauty starts from within.*

My shortest child would have liked to have grown taller. My son would have liked to have been older – or at least for me to have given birth to a little brother. My middle child has actually dyed her hair black to cover the bronze streak of hair. Over the years, the short one has embraced being short. When she wants to be 'taller', she has a closet full of shoes with high heels. My son has accepted that I, his mother, am **NOT** having any more children. However, he has a nephew he's been around since birth, and they adore one another. In this age of hair-coloring and streaking, my middle daughter is proud to have her naturally-bronze streak, and she does an excellent job of styling her hair to show it off.

My point is this: It takes time, and time should not be rushed. 'It' doesn't happen just because you want it to. Restoring is about rebuilding, and in doing so, one must learn how to adapt, adjust, and accept. My children realized in their own time that what they wanted and what was realistic did not always align the way they wanted them to. What did they do? They made the best of what they were given and found some things to complement them – and they are happier and far more content.

I think of my life in terms of when my children were born and watching them grown into adulthood. I remember how excited I was to see each of them take their first steps and grow in their first tooth. I remember their first day of school. I remember teaching them how to ride a bike and the first time I let go to allow them to ride on their own. I remember cleaning up their bumps and bruises. I remember their first loves and first heartaches. I remember their recitals, pageants, debates, proms, and graduations. I remember the births of their own children.

Restoring the Whole in My Soul

It was a long process from birth to adulthood. They didn't walk, talk, or run at the same time. They didn't start school or learn at the same pace or in the same way. Despite their trials and triumphs, I love them unconditionally. I don't care how long it took them to do certain things: I'm pleased they stayed the course to get it done.

In the case of abuse – physical or otherwise – it typically didn't happen overnight. I believe we put far too much pressure on ourselves and others to have a belief that we will "get over it" overnight. Just as there was a process to being victimized, there is a process to overcome it. Trust the process. Believe that you can and will be restored to a place of happiness, peace, and joy. Know that romantic love can happen, but also understand that in order to truly love another person, you must first learn to love yourself **AND** establish a set of standards and boundaries.

I hope this book brought about some reflections, affirmations, and direction as you go through life's journey. Never run someone else's race. Never allow your voice to be silenced. You were given your experiences for a reason – a purpose. Always know that your story may be difficult and uncomfortable to hear. I always counteract that by saying, "If it's difficult and uncomfortable for you to **hear**, imagine how it must have felt to be the one who **lived** it." Let your adversities be the fuel to revive your mind, body, and spirit into the restored vessel of love and light you are destined to be.

Restoring the Whole in My Soul

RESTORATION NOTES

_____

_____

_____

_____

_____

_____

_____

_____

_____

_____

_____

_____

_____

_____

_____

_____

_____

_____

_____

_____

_____

_____

Joyce L. Kyles

About the Author

Joyce L. Kyles is a graduate of Arkansas State University. She is the Executive Director of Walking Into A New Life, Inc., a non-profit organization whose mission is to stop domestic violence and help stabilize victims. Joyce is a nationally credentialed speaker, trainer, facilitator, author, and panelist who routinely hosts events designed to educate, inspire, and inform communities about the importance of establishing holistic health and wellness, self-worth, and tangible self-sufficiency.

Joyce has received a number of awards and acknowledgments for her efforts as an entrepreneur, advocate, and survivor of domestic violence and sexual assault. She works with a number of individuals, businesses and organizations – both locally and nationally – and promotes a series of Men Against Domestic Violence initiatives through her non-profit.

Restoring the Whole in My Soul

She is a graduate of the Praxis International ALC training program and is a Certified Assessor to use the Danger Assessment Scoring Sheet for female victims of abuse. She has also served as a weekly special guest on a local radio talk show to share her insights. She now hosts a radio show called "Boots on the Ground" to bring attention to individuals, businesses, and organizations that serve as our unsung heroes in their respective communities.

She is a member of the Tennessee Coalition to End Domestic and Sexual Violence and the VOICES Speakers Bureau of Memphis and Shelby Counties. Her past experiences include: Victim Advocate with the Shelby County Government's Crimes Victims Center, Mentor for Big Brothers/Big Sisters, and Caseworker for Shelby County Juvenile Court. She also served as an active member of the National Coalition of 100 Black Women, Inc. – Memphis Chapter for four years, using her talents as the Public Relations Director and Chairperson for its Annual Young Women of Excellence Conference for two years.

Joyce is currently married to Jason Kyles and has three beautiful children from a previous marriage.

Joyce L. Kyles

Connect and Contact Information

For Bookings and Media Interviews:

Website: www.joycekyles.com

Email: joyce@joycekyles.com

Connect with Joyce:

Facebook: www.facebook.com/joycelkyles

Twitter: @joycekyles

Instagram: @joycekyles

Pinterest: @joycekyles

Restoring the Whole in My Soul

Joyce L. Kyles